HARD RESET

Your Life to Freedom

CHARITY MORSEY

WESTBOW
PRESS®
A DIVISION OF THOMAS NELSON
& ZONDERVAN

WestBow Press books may be ordered through booksellers or by contacting:

WestBow Press
A Division of Thomas Nelson & Zondervan
1663 Liberty Drive
Bloomington, IN 47403
www.westbowpress.com
844-714-3454

ISBN: 979-8-3850-2584-8 (sc)
ISBN: 979-8-3850-2586-2 (hc)
ISBN: 979-8-3850-2585-5 (e)

Library of Congress Control Number: 2024910547

Print information available on the last page.

WestBow Press rev. date: 06/03/2024

Contents

Hard Reset: Costa Rica

Hard Reset: London

Hard Reset: Paris

Hard Reset: Bali, Baja, California

Hard Reset: Revitalized, Restored, and Renewed

Notes

About the Author, Charity Morsey

Charity Morsey is a national security expert, professor, diplomat, and author. She has traveled to over thirty countries during her career and speaks five languages. She has a Bachelor of Arts in International Affairs and a Master's Degree in Public Policy from Pepperdine University. Presently, Morsey volunteers as a motivational speaker at local women's shelters and recovery homes, and loves watching her two boys excel in life and in sports. She founded Generation for Freedom, a non-profit committed to raising up the next generation for lives of purpose and service through women and children breaking free from the chains of poverty and slavery.

Growing up, Charity Morsey's parents ran a home for those in need. "I was raised to live out my name *Charity* through my life's calling," she says. Over the last two decades of her impressive public service career, Morsey has acted as the first special assistant on international affairs for the Science and Technology Directorate at the U.S. Department of Homeland Security and a senior policy advisor on nuclear nonproliferation at the U.S. Department of Energy under President George W. Bush. She also served as an analyst in the California Governor's Office of Homeland Security.

It was through this work that she learned about the impact of human trafficking and slave labor on women and children, which inspired her to launch her own non-profit. Generation for Freedom is developing a safe house for survivors of human trafficking and other forms of slavery. They also provide services to reconstruct and restore lives, while cultivating a community that helps people rebuild their self-worth. Morsey says, "I'm inspired by the women who take bold steps to break free from the cycle of human trafficking. Freedom takes flight when we are empowered."

GENERATIONFORFREEDOM.COM @GENERATIONFORFREEDOM

Introduction

Seven years ago, before anyone ever thought of "the cloud," my phone screen went blank. In fact, it was black and it shut down completely. My contacts, my data, all my photos, projects, and passwords were all erased. I did a Hard Reset to fix my frozen phone; but, instead of resurrecting my data life, it wiped the phone clean. It was a blank slate, a hard reset. Everything was gone. My whole life was wiped away by the push of a button. I was devastated.

Wait—what? How did this happen? Did I *Reset* it? I had wiped the entire phone clean? No memory? No data? No photos? No calendar? Everything important to me was gone. I was about to board a plane to Costa Rica and my phone had become frozen, so I knew I had to reset it… It was going to be my first Christmas alone, divorced, and without my children for the holiday, so I decided to travel to Costa Rica. I couldn't imagine that in one moment my life would reset, personally, and now on my phone. As I waited to board the plane I asked myself, was this HARD RESET a blessing in disguise?

Yes, I affirmed. I am a blank screen now. It was there in the airport that I realized I had to re-start my life over. Re-build it, re-write it, restore it, and RESET it. I knew that I could not let the fear of starting over grip me, and that this hard reset would be okay, better somehow. In my vulnerability, I would lose the past, be in the present moment, and step into the courage of resetting myself towards a new future. I decided at that Reset moment that I would learn from the past, and not live in it. From now on, I said to myself, I am going to live purposefully in the present. Taking a *Hard Reset* in my life and starting fresh has been the most freeing and gratifying life choice I have ever made!

Hard Reset, your life to freedom!

Chapter 1

Introduction:
What Is a Hard Reset?

Everything in our technical modern world has a reset button. Most major electronics, appliances, and household items, have a reset button. Reset is a universal need and has a specific purpose.

We think as human beings that we don't have the capacity to hit a reset button, for ourselves, to start life over. Can we actually have a do-over, is it possible?

I'm here to tell you that if objects can be reset, so can we!

Imagine if you could have a do-over in life. What if every time you thought you wanted to start over, you could? Yes, you can, and yes, you should push the reset button in your own life as many times as you need to!

It's simple to push a button, but hard to retrain your mind. It's a choice. Sometimes you need to hit the reset button every day, possibly every hour, and on some days, every minute. Why? Because the mind and the heart are the control panels of the soul. We have the choice to create, build, and design who we are, at any given moment. **Why not**

recreate your life, hard reset it, and start over? What can you imagine? Who would you like to be? What are your dreams?

Start fresh, choose to have a do-over, and wipe the slate clean with a hard reset, it's never too late to get started!

Over the next 30 days, immerse yourself in the wisdom of these 30 chapters. Embrace the three Reset tips each day, as outlined in this book, and witness how they pave the way for a life of profound freedom and liberation. You are merely a month away from unlocking a brand-new existence, brimming with possibilities and untapped potential.

My hope is that by reading this book your life will be changed. As I share my journey, may it motivate you and encourage you to start your own Hard Reset to a life of freedom.

Chapter 2

Look Up, Look Ahead

"Fearlessness is like a muscle. The more I exercise it the more natural it becomes."
—Arianna Huffington

I consider myself a water lover, even a mermaid. I grew up swimming most of my life, and I love the water, so naturally I pretended to be a mermaid most of my childhood. Feeling like a carefree mermaid as a child was part of the essence of who I was, so I thought. So naturally, I thought that as an adult mermaid, that I would love scuba diving. I had enjoyed snorkeling and I didn't really know the difference, but I knew I wanted to be scuba-certified.

Every year on my birthday, I make big life goals. Goals that help me conquer a fear, or are out of my usual comfort zone. So on my 40th birthday, I decided that I would become deep-water scuba-certified. Thinking I would be a natural in the water, I was shocked when I failed to get scuba-certified. In fact, I got flunked on my first weekend in the ocean. My fear of breathing underwater woke me up to the reality that I'm not an easy-going seafaring mermaid. I was not brave at all, I was more terrified than I could imagine of swimming in the deep dark ocean. The Pacific Ocean definitely wasn't the same as a clear blue pool.

My first scuba lesson started in the pool, with a thick constricting wetsuit, a heavy scuba tank, a stiff rubber mouthpiece, a weighted vest, and big fins - hardly mermaid-ish. I was dressed and ready to go. I thought, how hard can this be? It's just swimming in a pool. I got into the pool, and as I went under the water with all the equipment on I freaked out! It was hard mentally to rely on a plastic breathing apparatus, even in three feet of water. I kept thinking to myself, I can't breathe, I can't breathe. After three days of crying during my lessons, the instructor looked me straight in the eyes and said, "You need some serious help to get over your fear of breathing under water." "What?" I said. "I'm a mermaid!" He laughed. "Um, yeah, I know that hat you wear every day to class says, 'I'm a Mermaid' on it, but you are far from it, my dear." He continued, "You can't even go underwater five feet deep in the pool, how are you going to do it in the ocean? Maybe you should stick to swimming in a pool or strolling on land."

After he said that to me, I decided not to give up! I completed all my pool classes. But, somehow I didn't realize that my fear of not being able to breathe underwater was still stuck deep inside of me. After the pool test, was the ocean test, to prove what I learned in the pool. The day of the ocean test was here and there were eight of us ready for testing. I looked out from the boat at the Pacific and thought, what happened to the clear waters and sun? It was a dark, cloudy, and windy day. The boat stopped at the 40-foot depth mark, and one person at a time went to the edge of the boat and jumped. Seven scuba divers jumped, but not me. I was paralyzed. I kept looking at the dark water, and psyching myself out! My instructor yelled at me from the ocean, "Jump," so after five minutes of what could have been years, I held my breath and jumped.

4

I started hyperventilating the moment I hit the water, opposite of what I was trained to do!

Once I was in the water it was overwhelming, I kept taking short breaths when I should have been taking slow deep breaths. I panicked and pulled off my mask crying. The instructor decided to try a new method with me, he said, "Don't think about how deep it is." Trying to distract myself from the fear, I grabbed a piece of tall seaweed underwater and started counting each leaf as I descended down. I counted seven seaweed leaves and then I shot up to the top of the surface crying. I thought I was really deep at ten feet down; but, to my surprise it was only three feet. I was basically at the shallow end of the pool. My fear of being in the dark water and not being able to see anything was terrifying. I felt blind and extremely uncomfortable in this foreign mermaid environment of the sea. At least in the pool I had visibility. My instructor heard a woman yelling from the side of the boat, "Charity you can do it!" Then, he said, "Who is that?" "Is that your life coach?" Gasping for air, I said, "No, it's my mom!"

After three days of ocean testing I couldn't even pass phase one. As I was mentally processing this failure, my instructor said, "LOOK, I'm going to suggest that if you really want to scuba dive, you get a private instructor and go to the Florida Keys. The water there is warm and clear, so take some time there to pull yourself together, Mermaid."

So what did I do? I went to the Florida Keys. This was my chance to accomplish my birthday goal of getting deep-water scuba certified by the age of forty. And I did it! Now, how did a girl who considered herself a water lover and a mermaid get over her fears of swimming in the deep parts of the ocean? I learned how to breathe sixty feet below the ocean surface. Simply put—I looked up and Hard Reset.

How did I Reset? I looked up every three feet through the crystal clear blue water to the sky. I looked up at the sun when I thought I could go no further, I looked up again and again reminding myself "I'm okay." As I went deeper I focused on the colorful fish swimming and beautiful seaweed flowing in the mild current so succinctly in perfect harmony.

And before I knew it, I was sixty feet below the surface. The water was clear, warm, and the view was amazing. I felt peaceful, and I realized I was going to be okay. I learned to look up, breathe, reset, and look forward. Getting scuba certified was a major life lesson and I learned a lot about myself through this challenge.

Now, let's go from the tropical waters of the Florida Keys to the mountains of Mammoth in California. I thought I would hate skiing in the cold because I'm a mermaid. Yet to my surprise, thanks to a ski lesson with twenty other adults, I found out I had clearly been missing out on the thrill and all the fun snow skiing offers. Who knew the snow wasn't a place to be cold and miserable? Trees weren't meant for crashing into- they were meant to be zig-zagged around with skis. And ice-capped mountains were not only meant to be places of extraordinarily scary heights, but they were also meant to jump off into with sheer exhilaration and joy. The white majesty of the snow on a blue-sky day was absolutely refreshing and magical.

During this ski lesson, I learned that to be successful at skiing, I needed to do only two things. First and foremost, you must always *look up, and look forward.* Let the direction of your head guide the direction of your body, and you will never crash. Quite often my instructor screamed, "Look up! Where your focus goes, you go!" Second, and just as important, you must breathe and breathe deeply, especially when you become fearful or hesitant to take the next jump in. Whether it is in the ocean depths or skiing down a mountain, I learned the same lesson, to look up and look ahead.

The lessons I learned in scuba diving and skiing are profound life lessons. To be intentional, confident, and at peace with yourself, you must look up, and look ahead. In every sport, and in the game of life, where your focus goes, you go, don't look back. Where your eyes are looking, your heart and soul will follow. The choice is yours to look up or down. . .*Look up and lift your spirits.* Let's get going!

Reset Tips:

1. Take up a new hobby or sport, especially one that you are not inclined to do. You will learn new things about yourself by this challenge.
2. Use your momentum to move forward through obstacles. Don't look back.
3. Look up, Reset, and Look Ahead.

Summary:

Trying a new challenge can be small and affordable, and even a memorable lesson. For example, my personal experience with resetting with a sport started by going to a spin cycle class. Riding a bike indoors in a small dark room with thirty other people seemed crazy. But, what I found out, was that I loved it and it's sustainable. To this day it is my weekly practice. I use workout classes to process any triggers or negative thoughts that plague my mind. The instructors are like therapists to me, they always encourage and challenge me to take up more ground in my life and on the bike.

Chapter 3

Memories Are Mere Illusions

"The soul has illusions as the bird has
wings; it is supported by them."
—Victor Hugo

Memories are tricky, messy, and scary; yet, they are magical, memorable, and special. Memories are meant to last forever, good or bad, right? Why do we remember certain moments of our lives and not others? The mind is a powerful machine, and memories are just as powerful. Some memories keep getting played over and over. They are pushed into our subconscious or replayed, and sometimes the negative hurtful memories unknowingly get too much attention.

Unfortunately, the mind tends to focus more often than needed on the painful or fearful memories, telling the mind it's for the best. This is a natural self-defense mechanism that the brain uses to tell us that it's for our self-preservation and self-protection. But, really those old painful memories are not in our best interest. We *live* 90% of our lives by our subconscious thoughts, and only 10% by our conscious thoughts. On average we have about 70,000 thoughts a day. Yet all of these thoughts are not necessarily good for us or need to be addressed. The key is to let the thoughts that don't serve us, pass by like a breeze, right through the window of our mind.

We are never too young or too old to allow a positive or painful memory to take hold of our present-day lives. Having said that, it is important to not ruminate on past memories or place too much attention on what is ahead. Rather it is more beneficial for your overall well-being to "be" in the present moment. Being present for the time and place you are in now, allows you to feel all the emotions around your day, whether they are good or bad. Experiencing and acknowledging the moment allows us to grow internally, and let's the emotions and hurts pass through. Every day can be good or bad, experience it, and if something goes wrong, instead of stuffing it down, acknowledge it and reset it. Acknowledging that moment gives it validity. Don't be afraid to confess to yourself the feelings you felt, and feel them. Otherwise, you might become emotionally numb inside and paralyzed. Without expression, there can be depression. Seeing the truth and facing it, helps you reset.

Are you paralyzed by an old memory, good or bad? Are you caught in a painful memory? Has a year gone by and you still can't talk about it, or all you do is rehearse it to yourself or others? Ask yourself, does this thought serve my highest and best self? It's just a memory, right? It's done. It is in the past, but it's controlling your present. What opportunities are you surrounded by presently? Being in the present is what you have right now, practice mindfulness. Embrace it, acknowledge it, and be purposeful in the present with those people and experiences in your life—now. When done effectively over time, mindfulness allows you to remain fully present in the moment, make better decisions, and foster more compassion for yourself and others. Let the present moment dictate your future.

To live in memories is to live in an illusion of a world already gone by, the past. Choose to live in the present to create your new future. You are the creator and master of your present moment, and your future. Granted, circumstances may change, and clearly the world will continue on its path, but that's not to say that you can't take hold of your present and your future. Embrace your expression of feelings, and be present.

Reset Tips:

1. Let the thoughts that don't serve you pass by like a breeze right through the window of your mind. Let them blow away.
2. Be open to new things in the present. Create your improved present moments and positive memories.
3. Embrace thoughts of gratitude and positivity to redirect your mind.

Summary:

My personal Reset. I go to a yoga class to breathe, reflect, and to be grateful for the here and now. The specific postures of yoga keep your mind working on the next position until it becomes a gentle flow in your body. You're not stuck in your head, you just have to get to the next position. The instructor doesn't give you time to think as you follow their instructions, the flow becomes a sweet harmony. At the end you rest quietly and listen for a word, it will come. I felt a breakthrough many times at the end of each yoga class.

Chapter 4

I Hated Country Music until I Understood Life Can Be Like a Country Song

"The greatest minds are capable of the greatest vices as well as of the greatest virtues."
—Rene Descartes

"Excuse me, miss, you are going to have to tell your friend there in the waiting room to turn down that country music on the speaker system. This is an emergency room!" said the triage nurse, who hustled various patients in and out of the Emergency Room.

"Of course," I said. "But, please understand that this music, is the only way I got my friend to the hospital." Little did the nurse know that, if it weren't for one country music song called, "The Winner" being played over and over on the phone for a thirty-minute ride with plenty of laughs, was the only way to get my friend to the Emergency Room, who might have died that day of an alcohol overdose. That song, that music, the lyrics, and the raw nature of country music got us to the ER that day. My friend was saved that day, not just by the medical staff, but by the lyrics was so desperately needed. The music was a temporary reset.

11

Here are the lyrics to the song:

The Winner Lyrics
Written by Bobby Bare

> *He said now behind this grin, I got a steel pin that holds my jaw in place.*
> *A trophy for my most successful motorcycle race.*
> *And each morning when I wake and touch this scar across my face,*
> *it reminds me of all I got by being a winner.*

Country music is an acquired taste, or so I thought. But, guess what? It's not.

It makes you process your emotions, and take an honest hard look at your life. Country music lyrics are about the dirty, nitty, gritty areas of life that might make you cry your achy breaky heart out, so you can be tough-as-nails. It's a reflection of reality. Music makes us feel different kinds of emotions, and country music lays out all the raw emotions, for us to see our feelings in their true entirety. No matter what our backgrounds are, we all have a past, and may be singing our own country song, unknowingly.

We all have scars, whether emotional or physical, some we are proud of, and some we are not. Scars, are a mark left behind, from a pain we experienced, both externally on the body, and emotionally on the mind. Truth be told, we all have scars, in our minds and our hearts. Emotional scars that have been put there by ourselves or by others. But, emotional scars, we can't see. Emotional scars live hidden, unhealed, and seep into our thoughts and minds. The physical scars in our life can be obvious; but, the internal emotional scars we can't see, and govern our lives more than we acknowledge.

Now, having said that, we can look at a physical scar every day, its apparent, and we see it. Physical scars leave their marks on the body, the area is closed tissue, and it is healed. But, on the other hand, the emotional scars, of our internal mind, might bleed into our everyday thoughts and affect our choices. These emotional scars sometimes have not healed completely, and need to be addressed. In some cases, they may need counseling, medicine, a recovery group, a community around us, or just a mindset of shifting, a reset.

We live with the scars of the past internally and externally, but we can't let them define our identity in the present moment, or determine our future. Emotional scars are left by the hurt we have suffered. Scars, both physical and emotional, are healed pain, and there is no reason to relive that pain. Use your emotional scars to grow. Emotional scars may hinder your movement forward, they may try to define us; but, only if we allow them to. Use your scars as a learning tool, not as a defining one. Take the time to acknowledge your internal scars, write them down, or share them confidentially. Once you acknowledge them and process them, only then can they be released. You have the power to shift your mindset and reset your thoughts every day.

Reset Tips:

1. The physical body heals by itself; but, the mind and heart need a reset to heal. Each morning say three things you love, and three things you are grateful for, it will shift your mindset.
2. Don't let emotional scars define you, your identity, or your future. The past doesn't define you. Be inspired now, and live your best life now.
3. The trials of life are hard, but reset is possible. One breath at a time, you can breathe through the resistance. Take three deep

breaths, and each time, speak three positive affirmations over yourself morning and night.

Summary:

My personal Reset. You can't operate in a vacuum, and you can't isolate yourself thinking things will get better, that's what I did. You need, and I need, a physical, mental, and spiritual practice of reset. So, I chose to plug myself into the church community, and women's bible studies, as well as to be consistent with yoga and exercise classes. The resources are endless, but the key is to start seeking help, it's just at your fingertips. Reset your mind and body, it will refresh your heart.

Chapter 5

Shatter Me: Words

"Words are singularly the most powerful force available to humanity. We can choose to use this force constructively with words of encouragement, or destructively using words of despair. Words have energy and power with the ability to help, to heal, to hinder, to hurt, to harm, to humiliate, to humble."
—Yehuda Berg

"Sticks and stones may break my bones, but words will never hurt me" goes the age-old saying. But, words do hurt and they can break your spirit. Every word, whether it is directed at you or meant for you, does and can affect you today, tomorrow, and forever - if you allow those words to take root. Take it from me, a survivor of my own internal prison created by others' words, and my unfortunate blind belief of thinking they were true. Words have power.

My name, Charity, is just a name right? My parents have told me that I was a gift of love to them at the time of my birth, hence the name Charity, which means love. As the eldest of four I was independent, a self-starter, and strong-willed. My strong spirit began at a young age. Oftentimes strangers would criticize my mom, telling her she needed to discipline my strong will. She would respond to them stating that the same strength you see as a negative will eventually be a gift to get her through hard times in life. As a child, she said to me, "Charity, your name means *love*, but you are strong for your own good." Still, people would say to her, 'Don't you think you should tame that wild one?' My mom would say "She's a child she will grow into maturity with her strength and weakness." My mom must have already known that I would need that fire, strength, and tenacity to weather and endure the storms that life would bring me. She wisely understood that to squash the faith and spirit of a child, could destroy that child's soul and dreams.

As a little girl, I remember playing in my backyard among the many fruit trees by the pool, with my German shepherd dog, Daisy. I would create and make princess castles out of branches in the backyard, and believe I was in far-off lands of adventure. I would write stories as a child about being a princess in distant places. My strong will brought me many corrections, but I was never crushed as a child and I kept my will of independence. My name gave me identity and my soul gave me strength.

Being born the eldest, and as a strong-willed child got me through life— most of my early life, until I finished college and got married, where words subdued me. I let other people's words and criticism define me. The words became voices of insecurity then they began to take root in my mind until I was paralyzed by fear and ultimately those negative words would destroy me.

My strength and will served me well through my undergraduate and graduate studies, most of which were abroad. It wasn't until I was married and freely gave away my strength and will to another, and that I allowed it to slip away.

Did I take responsibility for letting someone else's words permeate my soul? Not at first, it took over fourteen years to realize I had the choice and power to overcome them. Yes, I had unknowingly chosen to take the victim role. I did let them define me because I believed them. I believed those words, and I became defined by them. Words can become a prison wall that you build around yourself that will never allow you to roam free in the backyard or allow you to embrace the simple joys of adult life.

When we believe in those negative words, we play the role of the victim, which leaves us with a sense of emptiness and, a place of fear and depression. Sure, we can receive sympathy and find an excuse for every situation involving words. But, we are left feeling lost and without a compass only because we have allowed our inner insecure voices (words) to define us. That is the first mistake that's leading to a continual downward spiral of fear, regret, pain, or shame which paralyzes us from living up to our full potential. Instead of being the victim we should choose to be the victor.

Words kill, words give life: they are either poison or fruit - You choose.
King Solomon from the Bible

My mom's words were life, and others gave words that gave life and death over me. Words have the power to breathe life and to breathe death. We live and die by words. Words are written on our birth certificates, death certificates, graduation certificates, wedding certificates, and divorce papers. Words are etched in our minds like they are written on stone. Words are not just words. Words have weight and power.

Reset Tips:

1. Words give life; speak positive life over yourself, with daily affirmations.
2. Words give inspiration; speak inspiration over yourself.

3. Words are whole; speak completeness, gratitude, and love over yourself, and others.

Summary:

My personal Reset. First thing in the morning, before my feet hit the ground, I do my "Morning 3's: I put my hand on my heart and I say 3 things I love; 3 things I'm grateful for; and 3 things I want to accomplish in a day. Next, I read the Bible, pray and commit my day to God. I read the One Year Bible verses and find an application to remember throughout that day. Lastly, if I still have time I also use the Tony Robbins "Morning Priming" method and application and make it personal for me. The goal is to do some or all of these affirming power thoughts, for 5-10 minutes each morning before you leave your bed.

Chapter 6

Pruning to Perfection

"Am I dragging around "dead branches" in my life?"
-Joyce Meyer

As I looked out at the vast Napa Valley vineyards the green landscape was set against the magnificent orange fiery colors of the setting sun. The flawlessly organized rows of grapevines at sunset are still etched in my mind, but what caught my attention was the well-manicured branches, pruned to perfection. Why does pruning have such a significant impact on a vineyard? Why are the best wines in the world made from perfectly pruned vines? Why does the vinedresser cut the grape buds off when it's too early in the season? They relentlessly trimmed the immature buds that were depleting the health and growth of the vine. They throw away the dead branches. This made me think about my personal life and when my branches were cut off, my marriage, my job, my children, and my self-identity. I was pruned to perfection for a new life.

Pruning can significantly impact the growth and future quality of life. Grapevines that grow in the wild can begin their life in the shade of a tree or under a bush. The environment has an overwhelming role in the growth and life of a grapevine.

19

In its' natural environment, the grapevine uses a pre-existing tree or bush as its trellis. What trellis of pre-existing people, places, and support systems do you have? Are they healthy or depleting you? For a few years, the grapevine will grow slowly to establish a root system, and then it will begin to twist and tangle its way up the bush or tree trunk in an effort to get to the top and find a source of direct sunlight. In the wild, the grapes may be bitter or sweet, making them most likely not useful for wine.The vine that grows in the wild struggles until it reaches the top of a tree or bush, and then it spreads out to "steal" the sun from its host. Vines are competitive. If they don't grow fast enough to compete for nutrients their roots are weak. The sunlight helps the vine and leaves to grow, whereby creating photosynthesis process for the grapes. But, in nature, you are not always sure of the quality of the grape. Again, left to itself the grape could be sweet or bitter, as it draws from the elements around it. In other words, wild vines can be a mess.

In a vineyard, however, vines are firmly supported, fed nutrients, and a viticulturist prunes them during the dormancy of winter. This is the time for heavy pruning that will promote and provide the highest quality of grapes. When your life feels slow and dormant like winter what should you do? Look at your personal life and inventory the elements you are drawing from. Are they healthy or is the source rotten influences? You are your own viticulturist. If you don't prune the vines they turn into a mass of tangled and overgrown vines and branches that need to be cut off and thrown away for burning.

We all make decisions daily, some life impacting, and some are simple. Decisions as simple as where to get our next meal, or as complicated as a career change. We can let life happen and be dormant, live in survival mode, or let others drain us, like the vine in the wilderness.

Or do we choose to ground our life to grow productively? Where are you grounded? Where have you planted your roots? The type of soil and foundation you choose to grow in will 'show and tell' if you are healthy and thriving. You are like the friends you spend time with. You are a product of your environment, and you are a product of your choices. Life's hardships prune us wherever we are grounded and planted. Allow the pruning to change you.

Pruning, by hard circumstances, may need the hand of viticulturists. There are healthy resources such as: meeting with a therapist; getting plugged into a healthy community of people, possibly a church; joining a supportive organization, or a life coach or mentor. Just like a vineyard, it has a community of skilled workers, and we need the same tending to grow healthy.

May our life be like sweet wine from a healthy vineyard that others can taste and enjoy. This is when you find fulfillment in being the person you were originally created to be, a person who is alive and thriving. The process of pruning happens throughout all the seasons of life. We need to work through it one day at a time. Life is too short, and time flies swiftly!

"Behold, the rain which descends from Heaven upon our vineyards; there it enters the roots of the vines, to be changed into wine; a constant proof that God loves us, and loves to see us happy." -Benjamin Franklin

Reset Tips:

1. Prune - cut out the people, places, and things that cause you to be bitter and unfruitful.
2. Plant - your life and thoughts in good soil with people, places, and things that will make you grow.
3. Produce - don't just survive, thrive.

Summary:

I use my time wisely, by planning out a majority of my time for each day of the week. I do this by scheduling time with friends who challenge me in a positive way and add value to my life. For instance, by attending a Bible study group or having coffee time with a mentor. I schedule my workout times for my physical health and restorative mental time by reading, and walking on the beach. I plan time to be alone and to be quiet. I take one self-care day or afternoon to do this because life can be fast paced and I feel like I'm on a hamster wheel. Self-care is self-love and allows us to breathe and to invest in ourselves to reflect and refresh, to reset.

Chapter 7

Transcendence to Performance: Re-tape Your Heart and Dance Again

The most effective way to do it, is to do it.
—**Amelia Earhart**

When you watch a ballerina glide effortlessly across the dance floor in her ballet slippers she flows with elegance and ease. From the viewer's perspective, she looks like an elegant swan on a glassy pond, a portrait of the famous ballet, *Swan Lake*. But, how did she get to this point? The silk on the outside of her ballet slippers is soft, but on the inside of her slippers, there are layers upon layers of glued hardened cardboard paper, hard as cement. What a sacrifice of dedication and pain she has chosen to suffer for her beautiful performance in those battle-scarred slippers.

The ballerina has transcended above it all, in her hard-toed slippers, the unforgiving dance floor, with tired aching muscles in her legs, and toes cramped in her slippers. She denies the pain as she dances to the methodically planned and choreographed ballet that she has practiced numerous times before. The blood on her toes, with sweat on every inch of her body, with tears, she overcomes every time she fails and falls. She gets up again and again. At the end of her grand performance we are all in awe, and applaud feverishly!

How did she pick herself up each time? Did she cry and fall apart? Did she tape her toes while grimacing in pain? Or did she crumble up on the floor and quit? Did she watch her every move in the mirror? Or did she focus on all her mistakes? Did she wake up early and go to bed late? Or did she take time to rest, reset, and start all over again?

You already know the answers, we all know what dedication takes. She has grit, she has the resilience, and the strength of character to carry on and finish well. Only you can answer how you are accountable for your own life. Did you quit? Did you give up on your dreams? Did you give up your heart to despair? Did you take your slippers off? Or did you re-tape your heart and dance again? Do you know personally what it takes to transcend your pain, and your past circumstances, to go beyond pain and failures?

A choreographed ballet is a beautiful and magnificent performance. It took hard work, with multiple bandages, and grit to get back up and start over again. You are the director, the producer, the editor, and the choreographer of your own ballet, your life performance.

Reset Tips:

1. Rise above it all, and purpose in your heart to get up again.
2. Life involves the blood, sweat, and tears that will refine you to the most beautiful form of yourself.
3. You've got grit, strength, resilience, and the character to ensure your great performance.

Chapter 8

Small Choices Lead to Big Results & The 1% Rule

"The measure of intelligence is the ability to change."
—Albert Einstein

I'm not very good at math, so I don't like making a budget; but, I love learning a new language. I prefer not to do "to-do lists," but I do like to run errands without a list. I don't enjoy organizing my closet, but I do like buying a new dress. I don't prefer to get up early; but, I don't want to miss out on a delightful breakfast or morning beach walk. Do you see any patterns here? Am I making good choices? Can you identify? What choices do you make each day for your personal betterment, or to your detriment?

In order to visually explain the concept of making choices, and how one small choice each day, can have an impact throughout your life, let's look at how a waterfall begins. A waterfall begins from only one drop of water, that flows into a small river, which rushes under rocks, eventually making its way to a cascading and plunging waterfall. Each drop has a purpose. Each choice we make can be likened to that one drop of water that makes a ripple effect. An effect that can create the power of a rushing waterfall. When we repeat one simple good habit consistently that small choice and action adds up over time.

Now, let's look at the physical world, and how a 1% change can cause a different outcome. For example, when a pilot charts the course of an airplane, let's say from Los Angeles to New York, if the pilot charts the airplane off course by a small shift of 1%, it affects the final destination of the plane substantially. Enough to change its final destination, taking the airplane to Boston instead of New York. Over some time that 1% error took the plane off course. This can be compared to the truth that we too can go off course, when we alter our choices and direction by even 1%.

However, if we make positive changes or choices that shift us by 1% positively, every day for 365 days of the year, let's look at how much that positive change increases our positive output. For instance, if the pilot had increased the speed of the airplane by 1% all of the passengers would have arrived at the destination sooner. Let's look at this as an equation, the equation of .01 multiplied by 365 is actually a 36.5 % increase in a surplus, which has an exponentially positive effect on our lives. This means that by choosing a 1% positive change, you can create roughly 37% of a new positive you, by the end of the year.

What does the 1% rule mean in practice and in a daily application? To become 1% better every day, the small shift changes will add up in the end. This positive change might look like five minutes of improved outcomes. For example, five minutes of a walk or stretching, instead of five minutes watching TV. Or choosing five minutes a day to call friends or send a thoughtful text. Even better, what if on your drive in the car, you spent five minutes a few times a week learning a new language? Over the course of the year, you will have picked up some key phrases and a new language. Take a look at your weekly practices and habits and pick one thing to practice and affirm for five minutes of your growth. Set up your physical environment and social environment for success.

Your life bends in the direction of your habits. Your choices will pull you like gravity in the direction that you want to go. *Life does not improve by chance, it improves by change.* It is important to ask yourself what kind of system you put in place so that you have the identity that you want to be exhibiting in life. Little steps, done consistently, time and time again, compound into big differences. And not taking those little steps, makes the effect almost disappear.

When you do this consistently, every day, it may take longer to reach your goal; but, the compounding effect is that you are building momentum, and that is where the real value is held.

Reset Tips:

1. Take an inventory of your time, schedule, and calendar to make it purposeful for beneficial improvement.
2. Take 5 minutes a day, a few times a week, to learn something new.
3. Decide and execute your 1% change/choice for the year.

Chapter 9

Tug-of-War

"Change is the truth of life. The only thing that causes pain is resistance to change. The way to growth is to accept it and conquer it with a tranquil mind."
—Amit Ray

Italians in Rome have a saying they use when something goes wrong: *L'abbiamo rotto.* It translates literally to "We broke it." I never would have thought that such a phrase would describe the tragedy of my divorce. Experiencing being a single mother with 50/50 shared custody was heartbreaking to the children and to me. Yet, leave it to the Italians to make a phrase that sounds so beautiful, when it means something so tragic. The phrase, "*L'abbiamo rotto,*" we broke it, hurts.

Vows and hearts were shattered, broken pieces of the complex puzzle that could not be put back together.

In Italy, there is a fountain in the area of the Villa Borghese of Rome located off the beaten path of town. It would go unnoticed because its aged stone is not polished or grand. But, to me, this statue spoke volumes to my life, during my marriage, when my husband and I were working very hard while raising two sweet handsome little boys. At that time my husband and I both had very demanding full-time jobs. We both are very driven in our occupations, so the tug of war of life broke us apart. I look back now and see that the path of least resistance of being a doormat or arguing, both had created a tug of war. I felt deeply that if I didn't stand for my core principles I would be negligent.

While in Italy, the fountain statue that left an impression on me depicted a man and a woman engaged in a tug-of-war. They were standing with their hands clasped tightly with a little boy sitting on top of their hands. The boy had a great big smile and was eating a bunch of grapes. All the while, the man and woman were clearly distraught, the man was looking away with his mouth open as if he was trying to get his point across. The woman had her head turned to the side, resting on one shoulder. As an outside observer, I saw from a specific angle that she was crying and trying to hide the pain and tears from the little boy.

A decade after my divorce I stopped and remembered this fountain, and realized that I misinterpreted it. I only saw what I felt at the time of my tug-of-war. I saw sadness in the tug-of-war, over what I imagined to be the child because of my own perspective. While in actuality, each of the subjects in the sculpture had a slight smile because the tug-of-war was over the possession of the grapes. In our lives, we determine our tug of war. But, if you look closer at the statue everyone is slightly smiling in the statue. They are okay with the tug-of-war, for something as simple as grapes, even the little boy is smiling.

Just like the statue, our perspective should be for something much more sweeter than our own selfish will. It's time to reset our thinking on our tug, and our war. We should be more focused on our giving and reconciling with others. Forgiveness is a cosmic reset. In the tug of war in life, it's not a matter of who wins, but the outcome. Today our boys are amazing young men who are talented, gifted, and thriving.

Reset Tips:

1. Have a vision of the future, don't get stuck in the broken pieces of a tug-of-war. Forgiveness is a cosmic Reset button.
2. Remember your interpretation of your brokenness may not be true. Look back and pause, reflect take an honest inventory without your emotions leading you.
3. Find different avenues to rebuild your life. Don't give up Hope!

Summary:

My heart was empty because of not having the boys daily at home, because of sharing them with their dad. So, after work and during the week. I started volunteering in the community by serving in different areas. Later I began a non-profit, then started a few new hobbies. These outlets helped me with my physical and mental well-being when the boys were gone.

Hard Reset: Costa Rica

Chapter 10

My Metamorphosis to Pura Vida!

"Gratitude makes sense of our past, brings peace for today, and creates a vision for tomorrow."
—M. Beattie

Deep in the heart of the cloud forest, high in the Cordillera de Tilarán mountains of Costa Rica, resides a unique and rare butterfly called the *Blue Morpho*—or, to be exact, the *morpho peleides.* The rare *Blue Morpho* is native to Costa Rica and acquired its name due to its striking royal blue colors, but also because of its ability to metamorphose its appearance to match and blend in many different habitats. The Morpho has an exquisite, and unique camouflage ability to quickly turn brown or blue, depending on the region of Costa Rica. The butterfly also has a unique ability to fly hundreds of miles through various regions on one flight pattern, with very little food.

The butterfly's journey takes it through four very diverse climates of Costa Rica. I was captivated by its amazing ability to adapt and persevere in each climate and various terrains while flying hundreds of miles, it exhibits true resilience. This delicate butterfly revived me and inspired me when I felt very weary and fragile myself. I loved the beauty, strength, resilience, and fortitude it demonstrated. It became my vision for a Reset.

If you visit Costa Rica you will undoubtedly come across the words *"pura vida"* at some point in your trip. Pura Vida means the good life or the pure life. Locals use it as a greeting to imply "to have a great time, have a great day, and many times it can be used as any type of "hello" or "goodbye" greeting. You will hear the phrase whether it's a friendly staff person welcoming you to a shop, hotel, or restaurant. The phrase is so embedded in the country that it officially became a term in the global Spanish dictionary. The phrase is associated with the feeling of happiness, well-being, positivity, or gratitude; and, is more than a simple catchphrase - it's a way of being for the Costa Rican people. Yet, it's so much more than just two words, it is a way of life, a "manera de vida," for the people and their grateful outlook on life. Gratefulness is at the core of the people's hearts, it's the very essence of their way of life. Everything seemed simpler and easier when you go about your day the "Pura Vida" way. Everywhere I went the people were happy, it changed my outlook, and even my mindset. It was an unwavering attitude of gratitude for life.

When I was in Costa Rica I started my first hard reset. I learned two beautiful life lessons. The first one was from the Costa Rican Blue Morpho butterfly and the second was from the phrase, "Pura Vida!" I learned from the Blue Morpho butterfly which metamorphosed through regions, how it changed seamlessly with ease. I decided that if I took on that trait in my life, and the Pura Vida mantra mentality, then I would live my life with grace, changing as needed, transforming me into the best version of myself. My time in Costa Rica proved to be a time of incredible clarity, freedom, and happiness, teaching me to live each day with perseverance and positivity!

Reset Tips:

1. Clear your mind and thoughts each morning before your feet hit the ground. Make it a blank slate, and tell yourself exactly this: *I am loved, I love others, I forgive, and I am forgiven, and today I will live with purpose and be content regardless.* There is freedom in the flow of letting go.
2. Let go of fear and fly! Trust in the transformation process.
3. Each day choose to be grateful.

Chapter 11

What Is the Parasite in Your Life?

"Every man has inside himself a parasitic being
who is acting not at all to his advantage."
— W. Burroughs

What exactly is a parasite, and what does it do to its host? Slowly and effortlessly, a parasite, robs its host of its nutrients until the host can no longer survive. I learned exactly how this played out when I toured the rainforest in Costa Rica. As I walked along the lush green forest and dramatic turquoise skies, I was absorbed by the exotic sites around me; but, then the guide shocked me when he pointed out with alarm that one of the grandest trees in the rainforest was dead. How did this ancient massive tree die? The tree was hollow inside, and the dull gray color outside displayed its lack of life, except at the very top of the tree, where there were a few vines with sparse leaves curving toward the sunlit sky. The guide explained that there was no hope for this tree because it had been devoured by the microscopic parasite inside.

Unfortunately, over time the tree was being attacked by the parasite, so its defenses were worn down, unknowingly leading it to a slow death. A parasite robs its host of water and nutrition, doing its dirty deed in the soil by infecting the host at the root system with mycorrhizal fungi. A parasite will increase mortality.

The only life on the tree was the vines at the top that strangled it, along with the parasites that destroyed it from within. The vines grew rapidly taking advantage of its' host. Only a few sprigs of leaves were left at the top of the grand old tree, but in the end, death was imminent. Its' core was hollowed out from the bottom to the top, then the vines took the remaining life by strangling the tree. Parasites from within, and the vines on the outside destroyed the ancient tree. This grand tree standing majestically in the forest didn't even realize it was dead.

What is the parasite in your life? Can you identify what is slowly, but surely, killing your happiness, your purpose, or your identity? Is the parasite a person? Is it an addiction that over time, that will slowly rob you of your life? Is it your profession or lack thereof? Is the parasite your past? Is the parasite a relationship? Is the parasite your fear? Is the parasite your self-doubt? Parasites destroy you from the root system, devour the core of your true identity, and destroy the beauty and purpose of your life. What vines have wrapped themselves around you, taking advantage of you in your weakness? Could it be people who bring you down by their critical words? Might it be you're stuck in self-sabotage? Could it be an unhealthy habit that you repeat to escape, that strangles the life out of you?

Ask the hard questions, and identify the parasites and vines in your life before it's too late. Reset your intentions so that you can live each day to your fullest potential. You are a unique person, there is only one of you!

Reset Tips:

1. Identify the parasites in your life. Examine yourself and write out those three areas. Don't let it suck the life out of you.
2. Acknowledge the vines that have strangled you. Identify them and write out those three areas.
3. Now, take action, and replace the parasite and vines with positive intentions and actions. Seek professional help if needed.

Hard Reset: London

Chapter 12

Sparkle, Shine, Revolutionize

"You must live in the present, launch yourself on every wave, find your eternity in each moment."
—**Henry David Thoreau**

As I walked toward the security agent at the Los Angeles International Airport, she locked eyes with me when I approached the security detector, "Oh no girlfriend! You didn't just wear all that sparkle, this is an airport!" I had worn my usual travel outfit of black sparkly leggings, my gray sparkly sweater, and—yes—my glittery headband. I told her, "Well, someone has to shine, and I love my sparkle when I travel." She laughed and proceeded to do a full-body pat down since the metal in the sparkles triggered the security scanning machine into a raging fit of false alarms. Glitter, sparkles, and pink lip gloss all make me happy when I travel. The simplicity of knowing what little things make me happy, like pink lipgloss and sparkles, creates simple fun and joy in my life.

You see, I had an unscheduled work trip in the middle of a warm December month and had to leave Southern California, where I live. I bought my airline ticket without flinching, and notified my family and friends within twenty-four hours of my departure to England. On the plane I wasn't looking forward to going to the cold and cloudy gray city of London. I also had to finish writing my book, but I had writer's block. I couldn't concentrate, and I wasn't feeling inspired. I was at an all time low and feeling under pressure to complete my book. So, here I was in London for work during the Christmas Holidays. Not exactly my idea of a great way to spend the holidays - working. But, at least I could stay locked down in one place and write since London is typically always so cold during this time of year.

To my surprise, on my first day in London, it was a brisk sunny day. I had finished work, and I needed to write. I quickly jumped into one of the famous black Hackney Carriage cabs in London, and said "Pleeeaaaaase take me to a place where I can get away on a Sunday, and concentrate to write." When I arrived, I was surprised as I looked out the window, I thought where the driver took me was a joke. It was a pub. But, according to the driver, he told me, "This is one of the oldest and most historic pubs in the city of London, *The Mayflower*". He went on to say, "You'll be inspired here." Not exactly what I had in mind, but unbelievably, it worked!

The Mayflower Pub was built on the Thames River and was re-named after the famous ship that docked there on the jetty. You can actually spot the original 1620 A.D. mooring point of the Pilgrim Mayflower ship that set sail for the first time on its voyage to America. Imagine the history and stories it could tell of those who sat in this very place for over 400 years. It's been said that Winston Churchill, among other great statesmen, could be found at the Mayflower Pub, to ponder his thoughts in a dark secluded corner, overlooking the river, in an atmosphere that created some of his influential writings.

In fact, some historians confer that Winston Churchill got his inspiration for his metaphorical speech on freedom at the Mayflower. His speech regarding taking a stand for freedom states, In this quote, "This is only the beginning of the reckoning. This is only the first sip, the first foretaste of a bitter cup which will be proffered to us year by year unless, by a supreme recovery of moral health and martial vigor, we arise again and take our stand for freedom as in the olden time." He got his inspiration for this metaphor for freedom at the Mayflower which was part of the process that had lowered the "iron curtain" across Europe. Churchill used his speeches to emphasize the need for the U.S. and Britain to be guardians of peace and stability against Soviet communism.

Amazingly, what I thought was an unconventional pub, was a place of history that became an integral part of the world's peace and freedom in the 1620's. It was the perfect place in London to give me the inspiration I needed to break my writer's block.

Reset Tips:

1. Sparkle and shine. Find joy in the simple things in life that you love to wear or do.
2. Try new places, you never know what you'll discover, and you'll be inspired.
3. Revolutionize your ordinary life to extraordinary, be free to explore. Think of something today that makes you smile and do it!

Chapter 13

Childhood And Faith

*"Faith is unseen, but felt, faith is strength when we feel
we have none, faith is hope when all seems lost."*
—*C. Pulsifer*

Children around the world are unique because they all start with a childlike faith and curiosity, they trust easily. They are full of hope, excitement, and joy. I was in London working. While sitting in the business center of the London Marriott Hotel, I was snacking on appetizers. I couldn't keep myself from peering up over my computer to overhear two families sitting directly across from me on a couch. Both families were dressed differently, and were clearly speaking different languages.

One family was from England, and the children were talking about a silly ape at the London Zoo and their wishes for Christmas presents. "Mum, did you get me the drone I asked for?" said the red-cheeked little boy in red khakis. His mom cleverly tried to make him guess, she said, "Well, what I did get you is gray, it flies, and it is fantastic, can you guess what it is?" his mom said with a smile. "Mum, I knew it, you got my drone!" said the boy with delighted excitement and joy.

At that moment, I thought about how children at Christmas, have great expectations and wishes, they believe unreservedly. No matter what country you're from, at Christmas time, many boys just want the latest technology. They believe that their parents can afford whatever they ask for, like a drone, or computer so they will ask their parents with anticipation and full of faith about their presents.

Simultaneously, at a table diagonal from the Brits, a chunky and lively curly-haired six-year-old Italian boy dressed in green camouflage gear and Diesel-brand leather high-top shoes exclaimed, "*Gioco! Gioco!*" (Toys, toys). He looked at his mom with bright sparkly eyes, after asking for toys, then ran excitedly to eat the cakes and chocolates. I must have smiled widely because his mother looked at me and said, "*Il mio bambino ama la us chocolate e giocattoli!*" which translates, "Oh, my little boy, he loves his chocolate and toys!" Then I replied to the mother, "*Come dovrebbe*" which translates to, "As he should." Studying abroad has its benefits.

I couldn't help but hear the little Italian boy make sounds of "*mmm*" as he enjoyed his chocolates and chatted with his mom about his day and his wishes again for Christmas day. He was enjoying the simple pleasures of life like tasting chocolates and he was so happy believing that all the toys he wished for at Christmas would come.

Childhood and *Faith*—make the perfect pair for us to live our lives by. New experiences, the expectation of goodness, and excitement all exhibit childlike faith. The world of childlike faith and *joy* is a natural feeling in the heart of a young child. I found that true happiness can never be found in a person, place, or thing. But, rather joy can be found in the simple things of life like, a happy baby, a beautiful sunset, a piece of chocolate, a clean car, or a well-manicured lawn. If you believe in yourself and think about the beauty in your surroundings, all that you can be thankful for you will know that child like faith. Don't be afraid to dream, to believe, and to hope.

You will find the freedom to be content and satisfied if you can look at the world through the eyes and heart of childlike faith. Children simply expect people and life to be good, and assume the outcome to be in their favor. I am certainly not saying that being naiveté and being happy all the time are necessary. But, what would your day be like if you didn't have those negative preconceived expectations of people, places, or things?

What would your day be like if you chose to be hopeful with what life offered to you that day? What would your day be like if you enjoyed the simple things like a child does? I say all of this to imply that understanding this and having an attitude of simple faith will bring contentment to your life. Then with the freshness of a heart like a child, you will be filled with a joy that leads to a life full of hope. You are just one choice and one conversation away from improving yourself - your life, your hope, your faith, and your heart will thrive. Each day we can start over again with the heart and eyes of a child. Childlike Reset.

Reset Tips:

1. Have faith, and believe like a child.
2. Hope like a child. Write down your hopes and dreams in a journal, believe and take action. Start somewhere, one step at a time.
3. Find joy in the simple things around you, and list three. Be grateful.

Hard Reset: Paris

Chapter 14

A Life Worth Living

*"Every man's life ends the same way. It is only
the details of how he lived, and how he died,
that distinguish one man from another."*
—Ernest Hemingway

For a work trip, I went to Paris. Paris, day or night is an exquisitely magnificent city, and a feast for the senses. It truly represents the phrase *joie de vivre* in its overwhelming sensory overload with city lights, people, and food with its charming little boutiques of cheeses, wines, and bread. There you can walk, enjoy the sights, forget about yourself, and take a fresh look at life strolling by Parisian cafes.

As a writer, people had mentioned to me that I should explore the cafes' of Paris, and specifically go to the places where Hemingway wrote and was inspired by a few of his novels. On my first night in Paris, I experienced the famous Ritz Hotel, specifically, the *Bar Hemingway* at the Ritz. It is said by historians that Hemingway liberated the bar from the Nazis in 1944. The Ritz was used as a Nazi headquarters during the occupation of Paris and legend has it that Hemingway who was a war correspondent, accompanied the American soldiers to reclaim it.

With seven published novels, a Nobel Peace Prize, and all that money could buy, Ernest Hemingway was a legend and tragedy. He was adventurous and a romantic in everything he did, from his personal life to his writings. How could a man who had money, fame, intellect, and stature die from suicide? Maybe he isolated himself too much, and that caused his loneliness? Maybe his lack of zest for life after all his accomplishments was hollow and could have brought thoughts of depression? How would it feel to reach the top of success in life, and not have it matter? He lost the joy of life.

I can't help but think to myself what could have helped Hemingway to get out of his head? I know for me I will do new things daily. I will take a different route to work, and I will experience a new coffee shop in that route. Why? I might just discover something new about myself in that simple choice to change my ways.

Play a tourist in your hometown, take a different route in your day, visit a new coffee shop, try a new food, or try a new hobby. These are just some ways to get out of your head. This principle of stretching yourself beyond your comfort zone and your personal limits can help you reset. Try it, a new adventure awaits.

No matter where we are in life it is always important to reset your mind and set new goals that can inspire you to even more creativity, and to dream. Your perception of your surroundings can help you get out of depression or see life in a fresh new way.

Reset Tips:

1. Don't dwell in depression. Ask for professional help and find a community whether it's in a hobby, sport, or church group.
2. Find new places to visit, and break out of the mundane routines.
3. Invite trusted people into your life for accountability and support.

Hard Reset: Bali, Baja, California

Chapter 15

From Failure to Freedom

"You might never fail on the scale I did. But, it is impossible to live without failing at something, unless you live so cautiously that you might as well not have lived at all—in which case, you fail by default."
—J. K. Rowling

Penniless, recently divorced, and raising a child on her own, J. K. Rowling wrote the first *Harry Potter* novel on an old manual typewriter and became a multimillionaire. Rejected by eleven publishers, and friends who told her to just get a job since there was no money in writing children's books. Rowling did not stop at her first, fifth, or eleventh rejection. She eventually published *Harry Potter* on her twelfth and triumphant try. What if she had stopped on the eleventh try?

Life is full of *what-ifs*. "What if" I did try again, and not give up? Instead, choose to proactively say yes, fiercely and flamboyantly go against the odds. The tenacity of J.K. Rowling to go forward, not give in, or not give up is how she found the freedom to live boldly and successfully!

Did you know that some of the most successful entrepreneurs and CEOs were at one time failures, flunkies, or fired? Well, get ready for the best list of the worst flunkies of all time (I just made that up). Here is the rundown of Failures who launched themselves into success: Walt Disney was turned down 302 times before he could finance Disney Studios; Albert Einstein didn't speak until he was four, didn't read until he was seven, and his parents and teachers thought he was mentally handicapped, but he eventually won a Nobel Prize in physics; Vincent Van Gogh sold only one painting—to a friend—even though he created more than a hundred paintings that, after his death, were valued at more than $800 million; and Abraham Lincoln, was defeated numerous times for public office, had a nervous breakdown, struggled with dyslexia and had serious vision problems, but he became the 16th President of the United States of America and one of the most beloved presidents for his brave tenacity for freedom.

Remember, success can come at a price, the price being that failure comes along the way. We should see failures as a pathway to success. There is no success without failure.

As I sit in a cafe in San Francisco not more than forty-eight hours after landing on U.S. soil, I wonder at the landscape around me and think about what great writers looked to for inspiration after failure. What a surprise it was for me to learn that the famous Mark Twain was a writer for *The San Francisco Chronicle* —and guess what—he got fired! Aren't you glad I started this chapter off with the inspirational thought about "failure to freedom"? Or maybe we should say "from fired to freedom." There is freedom in knowing that you are good enough to persevere and keep going - even though your peers or your superiors might not believe in you - believe in yourself. Use your failures to launch yourself into freedom.

Reset Tips:

1. Reinvent and reset. Inventory your natural talents and put them to use.

2. Don't overthink, it's okay to fail. Reset your mindset to success.

3. Launch your failures into your personal freedoms, and pursue your dreams.

Chapter 16

Evolve with the Ebbs and Flow of Life

"Life is a moving, breathing thing. We have to be willing to constantly evolve. Life is a constant transformation."
—*N. Peoples*

Laying down on my yoga mat, the instructor asked us to close our eyes and listen to our surroundings in silence for three minutes. Stretching on my yoga mat and sweating, I didn't hear anything at first; but, after a few seconds, I began to hear the waves crash in the distance, and feel the breeze blow on my face. In that silent moment, I began to ponder about the ebbs and flow of life.

The ebbs and flow of life had almost destroyed me because I didn't understand how to handle the ups and downs of hardships and the happiness of relationships and failures. Our existence in life is always moving and changing. Seasons come and go because life has an ebb and flow. We see this exhibited in everything created on the earth. If you're brave enough to handle the constant evolution of the ups and downs of your life it will bring true transformation.

All of nature has an ebb and flow. Flowers open and close with the morning light and setting sun. The sun rises and the moon sets and rises over the horizon again and again. The tides in the ocean rise and fall due to the gravitational forces exerted by the earth and moon. Why did this thought come to mind as I listened to the waves break? I have sat many times staring at the waves crashing in front of me admiring its beauty and majesty. I started to ponder how the waves rise and fall as they break along the shore. The rising and falling of the tides symbolize the permanence of change, with the constant ebb and flow representing the cyclical nature of life's ups and downs. Everything has a season.

While on my mat I started to think about the core of the earth and how it related to who I am in my innermost being. For instance, the core of Earth dictates the expanding and contracting movement that affects our existence. The Earth's core with its intense heat has an impact on the surface temperatures. The core of the Earth has a pulse of ebbs and flows responsible for the Earth's magnetic field, and this also provides shielding protection for the atmosphere. The core is the innermost part of the earth's center. The core is the most central part of the Earth and pivotal to our existence. The core of who you are is the most important center of your life. This is why taking time to reset your core helps you to deal with the ebbs and flows of your highs and lows.

The human body has designed functions of ebbs and flows. The lungs in our body expand and contract systematically so we can breathe. The heart pumps blood by expanding and contracting so we can live. Naturally and effortlessly, the heart and lungs are sustaining us - keeping us alive. What would happen if your lungs didn't expand, your heart didn't beat, the sun didn't rise, the moon didn't set, the flower didn't open, and the tide didn't recede? You already know the answer—no light, no breath, no life.

A relationship has an ebb and flow, you are giving and receiving in relationships. Take in the good and get rid of the bad. For your best self, you need to take in what is healthy and get rid of that which isn't healthy. Accept what helps and discard what is not of service in your life. Let the good flow in and let the good flow out. Receive love and give love. Receive joy and give joy.

Reset, refresh, rejuvenate. Take in a deep breath and open up your heart, your mind, and your awareness of creation with its ebbs and flows. Overcoming areas in our lives takes courage to embrace and evolve with the ebbs and flows of life to transform the core of our identity, our soul.

Reset Tips:

1. Go to a quiet outdoor space or a quiet room, and be silent.
2. Listen to your reflective thoughts, they can be good or bad, and that's okay. Reset your thoughts with affirming positive ones.
3. Embrace your ebbs and flows and use them for positive transformation. Reset your core.

Chapter 17

Sand and Sea Glass

"Change is inevitable, but transformation is a choice."
—H. Amara

One weekend I found myself needing a complete change in my environment. I had become stuck in my mundane routines and was craving a new experience, or someplace that would ignite inspiration. As a writer, I sometimes have to try a new location, or immerse myself in nature to become inspired when creating and processing a new idea. I decided that I would drive up the Pacific Coast Highway from southern California to northern California to a quaint fishing town that was known for legends of mermaids and treasures - what the locals called "sea gems" - or simply known as sea glass - that was brought by the ocean for hundreds of years to the sandy shores of Pacifica, California.

When I arrived I began my adventure strolling on the main street of town by perusing small boutique art and jewelry shops. Almost every shop in town had one thing in common. They all used the so-called "sea gems" as the main objects to create unique jewelry and mosaic masterpieces of wall art that were shaped into hearts, birds, mermaids, and other ocean animals. The colors of the sea glass gems ranged in different hues of light and dark emerald green, sapphire blue, and amber brown. I couldn't believe the colors and smooth appearance of the sea gems that created such unique pieces of art.

Sea glass is refined, as it's broken down and knocked around in the ocean by the sand, rocks, and saltwater that churns it for decades - eventually it becomes softly rounded and polished sea gems. Only through this beating over time, sometimes hundreds of years, do the broken edges of glass become smooth, creating a beautiful piece of art, called "sea gems." Genuine sea glass can be spotted along many sandy shores around the world, and is extremely durable, making it wonderful to use in jewelry and art. Sea glass goes through a complete transformation. A transformation that takes it beyond its rough form to become a beautiful piece of glass. Sea glass is truly a symbol of resilience, renewal, and healing, since it has been refined by the beating of the waves, thrown against the rocks, and pounded into the sand. This process, which is similar to life, creates a beautiful gem-like glass that can be made into jewelry. I took one of the sea glass gems that I found and made it into a ring, that I wear to remind me, of this process of transformation.

What does the process of transformation in sea glass teach us about life? How do you use things that are hidden and undiscovered in your life? How do you use the broken and tumultuous turmoils of life to improve yourself? Are you okay to get weathered by the elements of life? Do you use the pain in your life to refine yourself?

Embrace the harsh elements of suffering and let them shape you into a piece of art that is uniquely you. Let the gems of your life no longer be hidden, but use them as a reset of beauty. You are a treasure.

Reset Tips:

1. Take a moment to enjoy the simplicity of nature, look for sea glass in the sand. Remind yourself of your beauty.
2. Take a moment to reflect on your brokenness, and use it as personal transformation. Get the help that you need for this process.
3. Take a moment for yourself every day, to pause, and reset your mindset.

Chapter 18

The Final Nail

"When we quit thinking primarily about ourselves
and our own self-preservation, we undergo a truly
heroic transformation of consciousness."
—Joseph Campbell

What does it mean when we say 'put the final nail in the coffin?' The body has died and is ready to be buried. It is placed in the coffin and the top is shut, never to be opened again. Nails are strategically placed in every corner of the coffin, and it is not until the final nail is placed that the body is lowered to the grave. There is no return. Throughout history, this quote has been used as a way of saying, 'That's the end of it.' Why do I use this analogy? It means, there is nothing more to do, it's sealed, and the finality is irreversible.

Is the final nail in the coffin forgiveness? How does this apply to us? We must truly bury and leave the memories of the past. Leave behind in our mind the pounding thoughts of the person that hurt us. Let go of the resentment and past failures that haunt you. Take a moment in time to forgive others and yourself. We must absolutely put the last nail in the coffin. Visualize the final nail and tell yourself out loud and inwardly that the memory is dead—it's done, it's gone, and it will never return.

Put that hurt, problem, thought, or pain in the coffin. Put the last nail in it, bury it fully, mourn it, but for not too long, and be done with it.

Reset Tips:

1. Acknowledge the pain and the past. Sit with it, mourn it, and then bury it.
2. Write what you want to bury on a piece of paper, and then burn it.
3. There is nothing more to do, it's sealed, it's final. Give yourself a Do-Over.

Chapter 19

Perspective Changes Everything

*"Love and Fear, the opposing forces from
which we shape our reality."*
—Edgar Mueller

Edgar Mueller is a world-renowned 3-D artist. He is the master of blending street art with concepts of optical illusions. His style of art creates a unique perspective for the viewer. His novel sidewalk art makes it seem as if the art on the flat surface truly comes out of the ground. Mueller incorporates the surrounding physical 3D items in the street into his artwork. The art blends so well that you can barely pick out the painting part of the artwork from the physical items of the artwork. Depending on the perspective of the viewer, it either looks real if you are viewing the art straight on, or if you look at it from the side you will see that the artwork is not real, and merely a drawing. If you're in the right spot looking at the painting on the ground, the painting can look like the edge of a cliff or a waterfall falling down into a pit of lava, if you're in the right perspective. Walk ninety degrees to the right or to the left and the painting on the ground merely looks like lines. It's the perspective that allows the art to come to life.

In the wise words of Mueller "In my paintings, I'm trying to question our perception of daily life by changing the appearance of public spaces. Playing with positives and negatives forces people to think twice about everything they see." Do you have a certain pattern in the way you see life? Are you blind to seeing great things around you? Altering your perspective exposes your vision to change. Changing the way you look at things creates a new perspective.

You have to practice being in a new mindset continually. For instance, break the habit of being yourself by trying new routines. Take a different route to work, try a new food, brush your hair with your non-dominant hand. It is only when you get out of your routine and comfort zone that you will have a new perspective. Be forward-thinking, identify how you can grow and see a better future for yourself, and focus on that better future. Focus on a growth mindset. It's all about resetting and beginning with a new perspective.

Reset Tips:

1. Determine your perspective, and change your mindset to positivity. Have a vision. Make a vision board.
2. Everything has meaning, see what is in front of you, and look at it with a fresh new perspective.
3. There are only two ways to live, either in fear or in love. Choose love.

Chapter 20

The Brain Is Invincible

"Transformation is not a destination, it's a journey
of continuous growth and self-discovery."
—*Tony Robbins*

Sitting across the table from the physicist for the U.S. President during my job interview at a tapas bar in Washington D.C. I knew from one question, and my one answer, that I got the job at the White House. Dr. Albright lowered his glasses and reached into his pocket protector to grab one of his thick Mont Blanc pens, and proceeded to guide his pen down a list he was reading to me, and asked me, "How do you feel about constant challenge and change?" And I replied "I embrace change and use it to propel myself to new heights of learning. I might be a policy analyst, but I am a sponge and can learn anything I put my mind to. Give me a chance and you will never doubt your decision to make me your youngest nuclear research analyst! The job was mine.

Our brain is moldable, pliable, shapeable, and workable. In other words, our brain is malleable. Challenging the brain to new sensory experiences and new learning is the best thing you can do for yourself. When you challenge yourself and even do something that you don't like, your brain fires off actively and creates new neural pathways and a specific part of the brain called the neural cortex actually grows. Think of the brain as an ecosystem that has billions of neurons firing at one another. Neurologists used to think that the brain could be likened to that of a hard drive whereby certain parts had very specific functions, and that if one part was not present or not firing off then the rest of the brain could not function. Simply, that is not the case. Today neurologists know the brain as something malleable that can be rewired to create new neural pathways. Think of the brain like the ocean: there are countless organisms and sea life that all make up different ecosystems which all work together in harmony. In the same way, the various systems within the brain work together to harmonize. It is not a machine, and it is not hardwired.

You're never the same from day to day, just like an ecosystem. We evolve and change throughout our lives. As we age we take life experiences with us, and some of those experiences are helpful and some are not. What types of experiences can we change? If so then, can the brain change? For instance, if you have fear, it is not permanent; it can be changed or rewired within your brain. Replacing a negative thought with a positive thought and replacing old fears with new beliefs can create improvements to the brain's neural pathways. We must cultivate emotional regulation. Emotions come in hot, so if you just keep letting them come in, your brain is being led by emotion. Regulation is necessary. You can regulate yourself by breathing, praying, and meditating. Emotional regulation helps calm the body down, especially through trauma. You have to cultivate it through positive affirmations. It is important to fill our brains with the right type of thinking. The brain is trained by the subconscious, which flows naturally. If you want to do something new, feed your subconscious mind with powerful affirming thoughts.

Meditative breathing eases our brain's electrons allowing them to easily flow. Anxiety leaves. Thinking speed goes from fast to medium.

Meditative breathing leads to direct change in the electricity of our brain, and can be measured by showing a relaxing flow of the body. We are electrical beings, and we need to bring the voltage down so we don't burn out.

Reset Tips:

1. Always start your day with meditative breath and prayer. Take three slow deep breaths as many times as you need throughout the day.
2. Your thoughts are just thoughts. Acknowledge them and let them pass by. They have no power over you. You are the master of your mind.
3. Every day think of three things you are grateful for and three things you love. Remember these positive thoughts throughout the day.

Chapter 21

Velcro vs. Teflon: The Attitude of Gratitude Practice

"Gratitude is a powerful catalyst for happiness. It's the spark that lights a fire of joy in your soul."
—A. Collette

Did you know that each person has an average of 70,000 thoughts per day, and of those thoughts, 80% are generally negative, and additionally 95% of those thoughts are repetitive? Let me say that again, 70,000 thoughts, 80% negative, and 75% repeated. As humans, our thinking naturally gravitates to the negative. Our brains are simply wired that way; psychologists refer to it as the "negativity bias." The negativity bias is defined as the tendency to pay more attention to negative information than to positive information. Here, more weight is given to negative experiences over neutral or positive experiences.

The negativity bias plays a huge role in our lives. It's why we can't stop thinking about that one piece of critical feedback we got from someone, even though it was surrounded by lavish praise. Bad thoughts tend to *stick* to our brains like Velcro more than the good ones do. Just like how Velcro sticks naturally to anything, so too do our thoughts get stuck, making them hard to peel off our minds.

Neuroscientists offer a helpful metaphor to illustrate the negativity bias. Imagine if, in effect, the brain is like Velcro for negative experiences; but, it's more like Teflon for the positive ones. Most positive experiences flow through the brain like water over a waterfall, while negative ones are caught, and stick with us every time. Basically, velcro sticks, and Teflon is non-stick.

If you feel like being positive, but optimism doesn't come naturally to you, it's time to give yourself a break. It's okay. It doesn't come naturally to anyone. Our brains have a hardwired tendency to downplay the good and hone in on the bad.

What can we do about hardwired negativity? Research shows that being grateful for just a few moments at the beginning of every day significantly improves well-being and health. A gratitude practice can look like writing down what you are grateful for in a daily journal to speaking thankful words of affirmation over yourself and others. The attitude of gratitude is good for the body and the soul.

According to a University of California Davis Professor of Psychology growing research indicates gratitude is good medicine:

- Keeping a gratitude diary for two weeks produced sustained reductions in perceived stress (28 percent) and depression (16 percent) in health-care practitioners.
- Gratitude is related to 23 percent lower levels of stress hormones (cortisol).
- Practicing gratitude led to a 7-percent reduction in biomarkers of inflammation in patients with congestive heart failure.
- Two gratitude activities (counting blessings and gratitude letter writing) reduced the risk of depression in at-risk patients by 41 percent over a six month period.

- A daily gratitude practice can decelerate the effects of neural degeneration (as measured by a 9 percent increase in verbal fluency) that occurs with increasing age.
- Grateful people have 16 percent lower diastolic blood pressure and 10 percent lower systolic blood pressure compared to those less grateful.
- Grateful patients with Stage B asymptomatic heart failure were 16 percent less depressed, 20 percent less fatigued and 18 percent more likely to believe they could control the symptoms of their illness compared to those less grateful.
- Writing a letter of gratitude reduced feelings of hopelessness in 88 percent of suicidal inpatients and increased levels of optimism in 94 percent of them.
- Grateful people (including people grateful to God) have between 9-13 percent lower levels of Hemoglobin A1c, a key marker of glucose control that plays a significant role in the diagnosis of diabetes.
- Gratitude is related to a 10 percent improvement in sleep quality in patients with chronic pain, 76 percent of whom had insomnia, and 19 percent lower depression levels.

It is clear, that the evidence speaks for itself, the benefits of having an attitude of gratitude are exponential and will always benefit your life.

Reset Tips:

1. Every morning before your feet hit the ground, say three things you're grateful for and three things you love.
2. Take those three intentions of gratitude and remember them throughout the day.
3. Before you go to sleep that night, remember how grateful you are for the day.

Chapter 22

Twenty-Four Inches: The Yoga Mat vs. the Prison Mat

> *"Man can preserve a vestige of spiritual freedom,*
> *of independence of mind, even in…terrible*
> *conditions of psychic and physical stress."*
> —*Victor Frankl*

Did you know that both the yoga mat and the mattress in a prison cell are twenty-four inches wide? Yes, just twenty-four inches. Yet thinking about a yoga mat generates feelings of relaxation, movement, and freedom. That is not quite the case when thinking about a prison cell, let alone a prison mat. Why do we get immediate feelings regarding each one? What's the true meaning behind a space and a place? How do you choose your space and your place?

Whether you have taken a yoga class or have been to a prison cell, that is just the starting point for understanding how your mind can be harnessed to propel you out of your current physical setting or emotional feeling.

My first time on a yoga mat wasn't exciting, fun, comfortable, or enlightening. I had signed up to go on a yoga retreat in the Eastern country of Indonesia. I took my own yoga mat, thinking it was cool. But, after twenty-four hours of flying with those twenty-four inches of mat with limited overhead airplane space, and taxi space, I was already over this little flying carpet machine that my yogi friends proclaimed would take me to new heights of relaxation and insight. Were they joking? Did I miss the news flash on the magic of the mat?

Jet-lagged and unsettled, I made it to the retreat space in Ubud, outside of Bali. The scenery was lush and wet, and I was ready to relax, not lie on a small yoga mat and sweat more than I just had in the last two days of travel. The yoga instructor insisted that we all start off the evening with a "welcome relaxation time" of yoga for sixty minutes before settling in for the night at the retreat. I had hoped that all my travel might have left me with food poisoning, so I wouldn't have to go to the class, but I had no such luck. Off I trudged to the bamboo hut in the rain with my luxurious, twenty-four-inch-wide, purple yoga mat.

To my surprise, after spending a whole hour sweating in a bamboo hut under the rain on that yoga mat, I was actually more relaxed than I had been in a very long time. I chose to change my mindset, quiet my thoughts, and stay still with the present moment for exactly what it was—that moment, that place, and that time to sit still and reset my mind and my intentions for the opportunity to rest and recharge. Reset.

Now, let's consider the opposite view of the twenty-four inches of a yoga mat, by looking at the bed mat in a prison cell. Somehow a prison cell doesn't evoke feelings of peace, calm, and gratitude; it is not a place of rejuvenation to the mind. It is more a feeling of being stuck, trapped, and shamed. But yet, it is the same space as a yoga mat.

You decide your environment.

Mindset is determined by the intention you set in your mind. It's your choice. Your greatest gift is your mind; use it to create your space and your place.

> *"When we are no longer able to change a situation...*
> *we are challenged to change ourselves."*
> —Victor Frankl

Reset Tips:

1. Your space is defined by your mindset, not by where you are physically.
2. Mindset is determined by the intention you set in your mind.
3. Your greatest gift is you. Use your mind as a motivational force to create your space and your place.

Chapter 23

Broken to Pieces: Just Enough to Make You a Complete Masterpiece

"Courage is the root of change. And change is
what we are chemically designed to do."
—*Bonnie Garmus*

Broken, sometimes just enough to break your heart and your life; but, it's also enough to make you a complete masterpiece. Sometimes a broken heart gets you on the side of a windy road in the mountains on the edge of a cliff, or a ride in an ambulance to the emergency room for crying too hard while driving. I loved greatly, and it brought me to my knees. I had loved others more than I loved myself. Broken, is this the way it has to be?

When you go through a crisis, either you're whole or broken. How do you recover during the broken times is what makes you whole, and a beautifully designed piece of art. Broken is beautiful. Your brokenness makes you a unique masterpiece of art.

Being honest can make you feel weak, but in the end it truly is the most courageous act we can do for ourselves. Broken is vulnerable. "Being vulnerable is the ultimate act of courage," according to writer Brene

Brown, a world-renowned author known for revolutionary books on vulnerability. If we can take all our broken pieces and put them together like a mosaic, they can be woven together to be a beautiful tapestry. An artist takes the time to redo, redraw, repaint, and redraft their art until what they believe is the image they want to convey.

If you're reading this, you're looking to improve certain areas of your life.

Like me, you're interested in *growth*. And what's the opposite of growth? You might say decay. But truly, it's stagnation. Staying the same. There's nothing worse for the human spirit than the lack of progress. But, to make progress in any area of your life – your relationships, your health, your finances, your spiritual awareness – you have to be willing to go on a journey with the ups and downs. A trip is predictable; a journey is not. A journey encompasses the unknown. And you have to be okay with opening yourself up to a level of uncertainty to obtain the growth you want. "Vulnerability is not winning or losing; it's having the courage to show up and be seen when we have no control over the outcome."

Reset Tips:

1. Broken is beautiful, it is necessary for courageous personal growth.
2. Change is courageous. Be courageous, stay vulnerable and teachable.
3. Life is a journey. Embrace life changes, it is the masterpiece of art that makes for the uniqueness of your spiritual journey.

Chapter 24

Hit the Mark, Release the Reins

"An arrow can only be shot by pulling it backward. When life is dragging you back with difficulties, it means it's going to launch you into something great. So just focus and keep aiming."
—E. Moizine

Nearly every culture in the world has used some form of archery in its history, whether it was for survival, combat, or competition. Archery is one of the oldest sports of art that is still practiced today. Archery most likely dates back to around 20,000 B.C. when early civilizations used bows and arrows for hunting. Around 5,000 B.C. the ancient Egyptians took up archery as a sport, and shortly thereafter the Mongolians perfected archery in combat to conquer civilizations.

I, on the other hand, took up mounted archery for the cover photo of this book. Life goals. And, not just any photo, it would be a photo that conveyed *strength, resilience, power, grace under pressure, tenacity, grit, determination, and focus*. What kind of picture could convey this, well none other than a woman riding a horse galloping full force, leaning forward out of her saddle, with a bow and arrow in her hand poised and ready to hit the target. That's right, to hit the mark, while in motion.

As I began to learn more about the art of mounted archery I took away some key life lessons, that at first impression seemed easy, but in reality, are hard to implement, but worth the hard work. How do we hit the mark with movement and power in our loins? How do we define our target, and how do we reach that mark? Stay in your strength while in motion, even when chaos seems to be the dominant force.

I first started on my quest to learn the basics of archery at an indoor archery studio. With my white wooden bow and hot pink feather-tipped arrows, my first lesson with a few third graders, it was a beginners' lesson of course. I learned how to have fun and hit the target, mostly because the bull's eye had a red balloon on it. The lesson was entertaining, but I realized I wouldn't be anywhere near hitting the target while galloping on a horse if I was going to just play around with kids. I needed to understand the mental aptitude it would take to focus under pressure. So on my next time at the studio, I decided to take a private lesson from the archer who owned the indoor studio, and wow did that change everything. The archer spent time working with me on my posture, position, and focus; and, interestingly enough, my breath-work.

The archer coach said, "You have to relax when you're shooting an arrow. You can't be tense. This will also help you in your day-to-day life as well. Now, I want you to inhale deeply when you draw the bow back and bring it to the side of your cheek, and then when you aim for your target - exhale as you release the arrow." I did exactly that, and to my surprise, I hit the target. I was shocked. Not to say this happened every time, but it demonstrated the necessary practice of relaxing and breathing; and, how this simple mental and physical tool of breath work provided precision. I knew I had to incorporate my new breathing practice from the indoor studio into my daily practice, especially when I kept hitting way off the mark. I learned that breath movement creates muscle memory, and allows the body to remember the correct form, as well as allowing the mind and body to be at ease.

The lessons I learned in archery break down to a few helpful insights. In archery you have a bow and an arrow, you can use both the tension and relaxation, leverage and release, in the moment leading up to shooting the arrow. Amazingly, you can be completely present with the bow, the target, and the arrow by quieting your mind, using your breath, to be intentional, in that moment. Being present is the greatest gift you can give yourself, not only to succeed at a sport like archery, but in everyday life. You can hit your mark and goals in life when you remain present.

After taking several lessons in the archery studio I decided it was time to mount the horse with my bow and arrow in hand. I decided that I was not going to have the time to get the archery part perfect, so I knew I had to get right to practicing how to hit the target while horseback riding. Finding a mounted archery arena and coach was not easy to find. But, I did find exactly that, a few hours away in the mountains of Southern California. When I met the mounted archery trainer she asked me "I rarely get requests for this type of lesson, but I was delighted that you came, this is not a sport for everyone or the faint of heart. I compete nationally in mounted archery as a sport year round. You've come to the right place," she said. In one afternoon, I practiced archery shooting while walking towards the targets and then I moved into shooting while on the horse, all while releasing the reins.

Yes, releasing the reins. At first, I was surprised that the horse knew what to do without me holding the reins, but the horse intrinsically knew. I wasn't sure how I was going to ride, gather my arrow, and hit the mark. But, I did, and it all came together smoothly.

How does releasing the reins on a horse, while having to hit the exact target, run parallel in application to our own lives? The answer, is only when we let go, of what we are holding onto tightly, that we find the freedom to hit the target. Letting go of the need to control, letting go of how to steer a certain direction, letting go of how fast or slow we move, letting go of expectations, and letting go of ego. Letting go of the ego, you will go, and you will move forward in life naturally, uninhibited, unapologetic, and un-resoundingly strong and brave.

In archery the pullback is hard, you have to keep your focus and your gaze forward. You don't look back, you can't look back or you will lose your balance and the target. This is a great example to use for the Reset in life. Pull back, embrace the resistance to launch yourself forward; but, don't look back, stay present, and use your core to help with your endurance and to pursue your dreams. Let go of that arrow and you will propel yourself forward to hit the mark in life.

Reset Tips:

1. Embrace the resistance. Pull back, and don't look back so you can launch yourself forward.
2. Your core values will hold and sustain you to hit the mark.
3. Keep your focus forward, release the reins in life, and go with the flow.

Chapter 25

Authentic Confidence

"Life is a matter of choices, and every
choice you make, makes you."
—*John C. Maxwell*

Remember the Bible story in Genesis about Jonah and the whale. Jonah had a high calling on his life to rescue the people of Nineveh, but he didn't embrace his purpose. He made choices that didn't align with his calling, putting himself and others in peril. While a storm raged, he chose to sleep through it, while everyone else worked through it. It wasn't until Jonah chose the right path, acknowledged his true authentic character, and embraced his calling, that his life had a purpose.

Every day we make choices. We make small choices and big choices throughout the day, the month, the year, and in a lifetime. Every choice adds up, and every choice makes a difference. Why does this matter?

With a Reset mindset and the renewing of the mind from the inside, not outside, creates truth and virtue. A wise biblical saying emphasizes that "Whatever things are true, noble, pure and lovely. If there's any virtue. Think about these things. And the God of peace will guard your mind." You have the authority to choose your thoughts.

A mindset is impossible to change without changing what fills your mind. Replace lies with truth. Confess what is true, and not what you feel. We possess what we confess. A godly mindset has to be filled and be fed with God's love. God chooses to love you unconditionally and eternally, therefore He does. If you choose to love unconditionally you will.

Now, maintain a list of all your accomplishments, experiences, and events that make you feel competent, great at your work, and confident in your abilities. In other words, Authentic Confidence. It is merely our perception of ourselves or our thoughts that cloud our confidence. So if we can address the thoughts or questions and thoughts and let them pass through. Then we can grow into our authentic confidence, by remembering those life affirming moments.

Our authentic confidence can always be present in us. It is merely our perception of ourselves or our thoughts that cloud our confidence. If we can address the thought and questions, and let them pass through then we can grow into our authentic confidence. Reset. Let go.

Words are powerful. Your mind will follow your words. It's the little rudder that moves a big ship. The words that fall from your lips will direct your mind on whatever course it directs. Speak words of life over yourself.

What inspires you? What would make you gladly get out of bed each morning? What makes you smile? What makes your life feel alive? Do you live for today or tomorrow? Do you live for others? Authentic confidence develops your choices and actions.

Reset Tips:

1. Develop a daily reset practice for the morning and evening.
2. Resolve and create an action plan for the month and the year.
3. Life is a gift, celebrate it, appreciate it, and give back, and serve.

Chapter 26

Worthy

"You are worthy of love and respect. You are beautiful, gifted, and intelligent. Don't let the storm make you forget it."
—*R. Davies*

Feeling worthy is a struggle for me. Is it for you? Do you struggle with self-worth? Once again, I found myself on a yoga mat - asking the hard questions.

I was on a weekend yoga retreat in Baja, Mexico when I had an "aha" life reflection moment. Stretching out on my mat, under a thatched straw hut situated over the turquoise Pacific Ocean, I was pondering my self-worth.

At the beginning of class for the retreat weekend, the yoga instructor asked us to think of one word that would embody our best and truest self - a word that we had struggled to believe about ourselves. This affirming word was to be spoken over ourselves all weekend on our mat; and, to be used as a positive affirmation to realign our minds, hearts, and souls. Additionally, if at any time during the weekend, our thoughts would wander into negativity, we were to say that word to ourselves repeatedly until those unwelcome thoughts went away. I came up with a word very quickly.

I was surprised by what word I chose. Without question, the word was "worthy." I thought it would take me a while to come up with a word; but, my body intrinsically knew what I needed to address deep within. I consider myself a confident and independent woman of value; yet, somehow my heart and head felt otherwise. Sitting in the quiet, with my thoughts, and having to actually be present with myself made me take a hard look at the core of my self-esteem or the lack thereof.

The weekend began a change in how I felt about my worth. It began in the silence of that mat. Sometimes every few minutes and sometimes hourly, a thought of 'unworthiness' would creep up quietly in my mind. I would be moving through a downward dog pose in the yoga class and there it was, I would think to myself, "You just did that pose wrong," or "Aren't your pants too tight, you should really lose weight," to "Your hair is so thin, look at that girl's long thick hair," and even "Do you really deserve to be here - you don't deserve to have this time to yourself, you're so selfish..." Once I learned to identify the stealth of those enemy thoughts -the enemy within- I took captive the thoughts with "I am worthy." And, as I got better at becoming aware of the -enemy of my thoughts - I learned to let them just pass through, and not even acknowledge them at all. Several times I found myself crying at the end of a class on my mat because the change in me was that I now felt as though I might be worthy.

It wasn't until the end of the weekend during my final poses that I found my mind had quieted down and there was no self-judgment - just peace. I had practiced worthiness on the mat. Now, I know why they call yoga a practice, because at least for me it is in the practice of going through the motions that you do the practice of the work within. Only when you practice how to move through the hard spaces internally in your mind, and externally with your body, can you begin to perfect your self-worth within.

Feeling worthy and self-worth are something that we can only give to ourselves. No one else can give it to us, and we should never allow any person or thing to partake in our feelings of worthiness. We are our own biggest critic, and can also be our own biggest fan. Feeling worthy can be a daily or constant struggle. Many times, just when you think you think you have been living a life feeling worthy, you have a setback, and the feeling of worthiness can go away. This just means you have to bring it back again, it's part of the refinement of your character. It's all part of the life-changing and life-giving process of transformation.

What is self-worth? Self-worth is the deep-rooted, internal belief, that you are enough and worthy of love and belonging - just as you are. If you are stuck in your life with your self-worth you can't soar to higher levels, and pursue your hopes and dreams. Stop doubting your greatness, build self-worth and embrace fully who you are completely. When we live in worthiness, we stand in our truth. Honor yourself, you are a treasure, you are valued.

"I urge you to live a life worthy of the calling you have received..."
—Ephesians 4:1

Reset Tips:

1. Believe you are enough. You are worthy of great things in your life. Set aside some quiet time to sit quietly and practice affirming the feeling of "I am worthy" into your worthiness routine.

2. Set the intention of love in your heart, and proactively live it out internally and externally for yourself. Self-love will give you confidence, and spill out into your own life and other's lives naturally.

3. Know you are worthy, and live out your life in worthiness.

Chapter 27

If Only... Hard Reset

If—
By Rudyard Kipling

If you can keep your head when all about you
Are losing theirs and blaming it on you,
If you can trust yourself when all men doubt you,
But make allowance for their doubting too;
If you can wait and not be tired by waiting,
Or being lied about, don't deal in lies,
Or being hated, don't give way to hating,
And yet don't look too good, nor talk too wise:

If you can dream—and not make dreams your master;
If you can think—and not make thoughts your aim;
If you can meet with Triumph and Disaster
And treat those two impostors just the same;
If you can bear to hear the truth you've spoken
Twisted by knaves to make a trap for fools,
Or watch the things you gave your life to, broken,
And stoop and build 'em up with worn-out tools:

If you can make one heap of all your winnings
And risk it on one turn of pitch-and-toss,
And lose, and start again at your beginnings
And never breathe a word about your loss;
If you can force your heart and nerve and sinew
To serve your turn long after they are gone,
And so hold on when there is nothing in you
Except the Will which says to them: 'Hold on!'

If you can talk with crowds and keep your virtue,
Or walk with Kings—nor lose the common touch,
If neither foes nor loving friends can hurt you,
If all men count with you, but none too much;
If you can fill the unforgiving minute
With sixty seconds' worth of distance run,
Yours is the Earth and everything that's in it,
And—which is more—you'll be a Man, my son!

Reset:

1. Don't wonder "If," do a Hard Reset on your life daily.
2. Stay true to your virtues and dreams.
3. Trust the process. Dream and believe.

Chapter 28

The Rear View Mirror vs. The Front Windshield

"There's a reason why the rearview mirror is smaller than the windshield-where you are going is way more important than where you've been."
—*Mel Robbins*

When you're driving your car down the road, do you use your rearview mirror to drive forward to determine where you're driving to? No, because if you did - you would crash. You cannot possibly know where you are headed by looking backward. Keeping this in mind, have you noticed that your rearview mirror and the side mirrors are much smaller than your front windshield? That's because where you're headed, going forward, is more critical to driving, than it is to look back or to change lanes. Driving with the path forward in mind, looking ahead, and being present, is critical for your safety and your mental well-being.

How does this apply when planning out for a positive route in your life? Simply put, don't get stuck looking in the rearview mirror. What has happened to you in your past, doesn't define you, and it's nowhere near as important as your future and where you are headed. If you feel stuck, it quite possibly means that you're spending too much time in the past, and not looking ahead. Frankly, it is much easier for the brain to live in the past, it likes what is comfortable. Staying in the comfort of the past, and on autopilot doesn't allow for growth. It is much harder for the mind to focus when it's stuck in a rut of complacency, or what we can refer to as "being on autopilot." Autopilot thinking is okay - to an extent. Did you know that 48% of what you do during the day is on autopilot. We might drive to the grocery store on autopilot, brush our teeth on autopilot, get dressed on autopilot. If we truly want to experience our growth potential, it is more beneficial to take our autopilot routines, and turn them into new habits for growth.

Neuroscientists have said that if you try practicing a new habit each day or maybe once a week, such as trying a new driving route to your grocery store, or brushing your teeth with your opposite hand, it will create new neural pathways in your brain. Pathways that fire off like electrical charges, and this firing creates new memories. New memories and experiences will create a new way of thinking and being, instead of staying in the same routines of autopilot. Wherever your attention goes is where your mind goes. Where attention goes, energy flows.

Reset:

1. Don't get stuck looking in the rear view mirror. Be present, look forward.
2. Develop an awareness of your thoughts and put them in their place.
3. Rewrite the script. Renew, refresh, and reset your thoughts.

Hard Reset: Revitalized, Restored, and Renewed

Chapter 29

Steps to Hard Reset: Your Life to Freedom

Be renewed every day by the power of your
thoughts and the power of now.
Do a Hard Reset one day at a time. Focus
on the good and what you can do
today and now. Reset requires new choices and habits.

1. Reassess your priorities, decisions, and purpose.
2. Renew and Replenish your mind with the practice of meditative breath work and prayer. Reset with positive affirmations daily.
3. Recovery is an important piece of the puzzle that makes you a complete masterpiece.
4. Rest purposefully, and set nightly intentions for the next day. Reset to positive affirming thoughts nightly.
5. Re-energize. Movement creates energy and makes you feel alive.
6. Refill with joy. It's a choice. Reset your self-worth with love.
7. Re-create. Realize that this life is your creation. You are the painter of your life's canvas. You get to fulfill your soul's purpose.
8. Restore your soul with the spiritual truths of forgiveness, love, and gratitude.

Chapter 30

The Hard Reset Daily Routine

The Daily, Thirty-Second Restart, Reset Routine: Every day before you get out of bed and your feet hit the ground, do your Hard Reset practice. Apply your Reset Tips by writing them out in a journal, and on 3x5 cards for affirmation.

Saying Yes 3x to RESET

1. Yes, I will forgive myself and others.
2. Yes, I will live today with purpose, service, and gratitude.
3. Yes, I am loved and will love others. The flow of life is easy when love is your way of being.

That's how the story and the book end. Rewrite your life. Rewrite each chapter and day in your life. Reset your life to freedom.

Ready, Set, Reset!

Notes

Printed in the United States
by Baker & Taylor Publisher Services